expressed or implied. Readers acknowledge that the author is not engaging in the rendering of legal, financial, medical or professional advice. Please consult a licensed professional before attempting any techniques outlined in this book.

By reading this document, the reader agrees that under no circumstances are is the author responsible for any losses, direct or indirect, which are incurred as a result of the use of information contained within this document, including, but not limited to, —errors, omissions, or inaccuracies.

Table of Contents

Fortnite: Battle Royale

A Fully Updated Secret Guide to the Newest Tips, Tricks and Strategies Only the Pros are Using

SGGFBR001

By

Secret Gamer Guides

Introduction

I would like to thank you for purchasing this book "Fortnite: Battle Royale - A Fully Updated Secret Guide to the Newest Tips, Tricks, and Strategies Only the Pros are using."

Fortnite Battle Royale has become all the rage in the gaming world these days. If you want to learn to play like a pro but aren't sure where to start, then this is the perfect book for you. You can learn different tips, tricks and strategies that pros favor and become a champion at Fortnite Battle Royale.

You may wonder how this book is different from all the other books that offer information on Fortnite Battle Royale. For starters, this guide contains all the juicy nuggets of information that you won't find anywhere else. We are a secret group of underground players who have spent hours on research and have interviewed different Fortnite Battle Royale Players. Unlike the other guides, this book isn't full of fluff or frills. The information is to the point and will prove to be helpful in scaling the game.

In this book, you will learn everything that you need to know to win Fortnite Battle Royale. It contains information on the various weapons, landing spots, building tips and much more. You can play like a pro within no time if you follow the instructions given in this book. If you are ready, let us get started now!

Thank you once again for choosing this book, I hope you like it.

Chapter One: Tips and Ideas for Base Building

In this section, you will learn about the essential tips and tricks that you need to be aware of to win more games in Battle Royale. These tips will come handy for beginners as well as existing players.

Tip #1 Know the game

The first tip before you start to play the game is to learn how the game of Fortnite Battle Royale works. Battle Royale is a free game. The game starts with 100 players.

When the game starts, you will find yourself on a Battle Bus. You must jump out of the bus and fly to a spot of your choice. Keep your eye on any loot and craft items and engage your character in fights. You must do all this while you make sure that you are ahead of the Storm. If you get caught in the Storm, your character dies. The last player standing out of the 100 is the winner. This is called Victory Royale.

Tip #2 Learn to build

The one feature that differentiates this game from all the other Battle Royale games is its building feature. A building isn't just a temporary base or sniper tower; you can build temporary ramps, walls or traps. In a battle, a quick wall can help to block the volley of bullets and provide you with cover. There are three types of materials that you can use to build - they are wood, stone and metal. Wood is the weakest while metal is the strongest of all.

Tip #3 Stay out of the storm

You need to avoid the Storm at all costs. Here is a brief backstory about the Storm. The world is taken over by zombie-like creatures known as the Husks, and the Storm carries them. Husks aren't a part of the Battle Royale variant. However, the Storm is poisonous, and it destroys everything that stands in its way. The idea is to stay as far away from the Storm as you possibly can. The map on your screen will show you when the storm is closing in, that is when you need to move to a safe zone.

Tips #4 Weapon rarity

There are various weapons in this game, and each has different features. All firearms aren't created equal in this game. When you find yourself in a tight spot, a good weapon will make all the difference. Different colors help to identify the rarity of a firearm. The color scheme to determine a weapon's rarity is grey, green, blue, purple, and orange. Grey color signifies common weapons, green stands for uncommon weapons, blue for rare ones, purple for epic weapons and orange for the legendary variants. The rarity of a firearm and its impact are directly proportional. The rarer a weapon, the more damage it can inflict.

Tip #5 Gather resources

Every player in the game starts with a pickaxe, and you can use it to gather supplies in Battle

Royale mode. You can pretty much harvest anything other than the natural terrain. However, it doesn't mean that you spend all your time merely gathering resources. You must prioritize the different items that will enable you to collect more resources. For instance, if you want wood you must harvest trees, rocks to gain stone and harvest cars for metal. If you want bricks, you can knock down a wall. You can destroy anything in this game to obtain the construction materials you need.

Tip #6 Chests

Apart from materials, you must gather loot in this game as well. The best place to look for loot is inside a chest, especially for rare and valuable items. One of the first things you will realize once you start to play is that most of the players tend to go for the chests before anything else. An exciting aspect of Fortnite Battle Royale is that the chests always spawn in a specific location. Once you memorize the sites, you can quickly get to the chests.

Chests are usually found in buildings like houses, towers and shops. Ensure that you check the basement and attic for chests since they are hidden from plain view. If you cannot access the basement or the attic, then you can build yourself a ramp or a staircase. Don't forget that you can construct anything you want in this game with the materials you harvest. Chests emit a golden aura, and whenever there is a chest in your immediate vicinity, you can hear a peculiar sound. So, you must carefully listen to the sounds in the game.

Tip #7 Build traps

There are plenty of traps in the game, and you need to be careful of all these traps. It doesn't end there; you can even lay out traps on your own for other players. Usually, there are traps near chests. It helps to kill the other players in the game quickly. There are different types of traps and different ways in which you can set them. Always lay the trap strategically so that you can kill other players in the game. You can hide traps at the entrance of buildings, set them on the floor or even the ceilings. It is entirely up to you, and you must think of creative ways to set traps.

Tip #8 Isolate yourself

Most of the players tend to head towards towns or other dense areas in search of loot as soon as they jump out of the bus. If you are a new player, then it is a good idea to avoid populated areas and spots for a while. There is no practice mode in Fortnite Battle Royale. So, you need to get a feel for things before you decide to be adventurous. Stay put on the Battle Bus for as long as you can and then dive out of the bus. Try to find an isolated area for yourself. Also, try to land on high ground for a good vantage point. Don't forget to check the map from time to time to see if the Storm is closing in on you.

Chapter Two: 10 Mistakes to Avoid

Fortnite: Battle Royale is undeniably one of the hottest games on the Internet today. At any given time, there are a couple of million players online in this game, and all the players are out to get you. The last player standing wins the game, so all the other players are your enemies. In this section, you will learn the ten mistakes that most players tend to make. If you avoid these mistakes, you will become a better player.

Mistake #1 Weak gameplay

At any given point in the game, 99 other players are out there to get you. It might seem a little stressful. It might seem like a good idea to hide in the bushes or one of the abandoned buildings you come across. You need to keep an eye out for the Storm because it shrinks the battlefield. A patient player might be able to sneak their way into the top 10 if luck favors them. However, if you want to become a top player, then your gameplay cannot be too defensive. Even if you manage to become one of the last players without firing a shot, you will eventually have to shoot the others to win the final spot. You cannot be the last one standing without making a kill. It means that you need to know how to use the weapons and only experience will teach you this. If all that you do is hide, then you cannot possibly learn the gameplay. However, it certainly doesn't mean that you must be reckless. Never rush into a battle headfirst as you will merely get yourself killed. Instead, you must carefully observe and pick your shots. Be prudent when you choose a fight, and you don't have to shy away from firefights. You might not win initially, but you will eventually learn. There are no penalties in this game if you die, so there is nothing to fear. Experiment a little, and you will learn along the way. Even if your character dies in the game, it only takes a couple of seconds to start a new game.

Mistake #2 - Do not forget what makes the game special

Fortnite: Battle Royale draws a little inspiration from PlayerUnknown's Battlegrounds (PUBG). However, Fortnite has a unique system that differentiates it from PUBG. PUBG doesn't have the crafting feature that this game offers. The ability to construct is an integral part of the Battle

Royale game, and you must learn crafting. For instance, when someone starts to fire at you, you can build an instant wall around yourself. The same applies to healing. When your character heals in the game, ensure that you don't get caught in the open unless it's necessary. If a hill seems inaccessible, then you can build a ramp to climb a hill quickly. You need a good base since it will offer a good vantage point. You can quickly pick off your competitors if you have a good base. However, you must remember that it takes a while to gather all the necessary materials and it might make a little noise too. Whenever a player builds a structure, it tends to make some noise.

Mistake #3 Mixing up the buttons

It is quite essential to have the right weapons in your arsenal. It is not just the right firearm. You need to have the right weapon at the right time. Firefights are quite brutal in the game, and you need to be quick if you don't want to get killed. If you fumble for your weapons in combat, you will get killed quickly. So, you must organize the inventory. You need to arrange it so that the weapons of the same class belong in the same slot every time you play. Don't get the buttons mixed up if you don't want to fumble for a weapon at a crucial point in the game. You can organize the firearms according to your preference or their range. For instance, shotguns can be first, then the assault rifles and finally the snipers. The only thing that matters is that you know the order. The idea is that you must not have to think too much before you switch a weapon. It will help you to save a couple of precious moments in the game.

Mistake #4 Stay in the clouds

All the players start the game on the battle bus, and then they need to jump out of the bus. You need to choose the right spot to land on the playfield in the game. Ensure that you reach the ground as quickly as possible. In the initial stages of the game, your aim must be to loot, gather supplies and collect the weapons. You must prepare yourself for all the battles to come and gather as many supplies as you can before the other players arrive. Never open the glider but instead, wait for it to deploy. The idea is to remain in free-fall for longer so that you reach the ground quickly. Once the glider opens up, you are an easy target for all the players on the ground. The glider deploys based on the height and ensures that you glide over a low-elevation terrain like a river or an open field instead of a mountain. If you trigger the glider, it will slow your descent, and you need to avoid this if at all possible.

Mistake #5 Audio Cues

In most video games, players tend to rely only on visuals to communicate. You will miss out on a lot in this game if you don't listen to the audio clues. You must listen to the sound of your footsteps, of gunshots and the noise the pickaxe makes when you gather materials. The noise that a character makes in this game is louder and more distinct than in other games. So, if you listen carefully, you can easily spot another player. It might be a good idea to invest in a decent pair of headphones so that you can hear well. Sounds are added to the game for a reason. Treasure chests and safes with the best loot make a specific sound. Players are of the general opinion that it sounds like a heavenly choir, so whenever you hear something like that, you need to look for hidden objects and chests. Not just that, you must listen carefully to the noises

around you too. A set of noise-canceling
headphones is a good idea.

Mistake #6 Lousy gatherer

You must stock up on supplies and craft material
as early in the game as possible. It is difficult to
gather supplies when the map starts to shrink,
and you have enemies nearby. It certainly isn't
convenient to run out of supplies while you are in
combat. You must learn to swing your pickaxe in
such a manner that it can exploit the weak point
system. Unlike in other games, Fortnite Battle
Royale doesn't have a tutorial, and most of the
players aren't aware of this specific feature of the
game. Whenever you swing your pickaxe, a blue
circle appears around the target. If you want to
cause maximum damage and demolish the target
efficiently, you must hit that circle. This tip
comes in handy when you need to harvest
supplies quickly. Whenever you harvest a tree,

remnants of it are left behind. If you harvest too many trees, the leftovers will give your location away to the other players. Don't leave a trail of leaves in your path.

Mistake #7 - Standing too proud

You cannot crawl in this game, but you can crouch. When you squat, it makes you a smaller target, and it is easier to blend in with the natural terrain. Also, it improves the accuracy of your weapons when you crouch. Whenever you use an assault rifle, make sure that you crouch to get a better aim. When it comes to the weapon efficiency in the game, it has a bullet spread or a bloom system. In this game, whenever you shoot, your aim is just one aspect of the equation. There is a random element in the game, and it means that the bullets don't necessarily have to hit the target. Due to the bullet-spread system, the shots can hit the edge of the target and miss the center.

The bloom is quite aggressive, and it often doesn't hit the mark. Therefore, to improve your aim, it is a good idea to either crouch or stand still.

Mistake #8 - Understand the materials

The three crafting materials available in this game are wood, brick and steel. You can improve your chances of survival in the game if you use the right equipment. Every material has specific features, and these features determine the strength of the material. When you build a structure out of any material, it starts with a fixed hit-point and, with time, the structure tends to acquire better health. Structures made of wood start with maximum health, but then they deplete quickly and reach the lowest health eventually. On the other hand, steel is the exact opposite of wood. Initially, metal is weaker than wood, it takes a while for its health to grow, but once it does, it has the maximum health. Bricks lie somewhere in between these two. If your idea is to block a volley of bullets, then wood is good. However, a wall made of wood won't stay up for long. When you want to build a tower or a base in the game, then steel is the ideal material. It doesn't mean that you should erect a steel wall in the middle of combat. Steel takes a while to gain health and, in a fight, the idea is to save yourself. So, you must select the material according to the purpose it serves and the time available. Another feature that you must be aware of is the visibility of these materials. Wood tends to have significant gaps in it, and it can give away your position to your enemies. Steel is not see-through, and it will provide you with a great spot to hide.

Mistake #9 Learn

Chests in Battle Royale spawn in specific locations. There are a fixed number of chests that appear in this game. Fewer chests will spawn on every level, but they tend to appear only at predefined locations. Initially, your focus might be to gather supplies and explore the playfield. However, once you get the hang of the game, it is a good idea to memorize the location of chests. Chests contain the best loot, and if you know where they are, you can quickly get to them before the other players. You must stay away from the routes that other players commonly use if you don't want to get killed.

Mistake #10 - Rob the corpses

Once you kill another player in the game, you can loot their body to craft materials, weapons and medical supplies. However, be careful of your position while you do this. Firefights are noisy and can easily attract the attention of others in the game. It is exciting to get a kill, but don't rush to the corpse immediately. Scan the location and then proceed. Ransack a corpse only when you are confident that no other player is nearby. Use the pickaxe when you loot a body. Whenever you pick a new weapon, you will drop the firearm in your hand. It will do you no good to lose a favorite weapon when you rob a corpse. So, that's why you need to use the pickaxe. The pickaxe is the best weapon to gather ammo, medical supplies and building materials.

If you want to play like a pro, then you must avoid these simple mistakes that most of the players make.

Chapter Three: Advanced Tips

In this section, you will learn a couple of advanced tips that all the pros utilize when they play Fortnite Battle Royale.

Tip #1 Build

It is essential to build in the game if you want to get ahead. All the supplies and material you gather will do you no good if you don't know when to build. Yes, you need to stay away from the Storm because it can make your constructions useless, but it doesn't mean that you don't build at all. If you want to take a couple of moments to heal in the game, then you need to construct a cover or a wall. It takes about three seconds to heal, and if you do this without any protection, then you are an easy target for your enemies. A single panel wall will do the trick, and it can easily block the incoming fire of bullets. If you know that there is an opponent with better weapons and health in your vicinity, then you must build a wall. If you want to chuck a grenade at your enemies, then it makes sense to do so from behind a wall. Not just walls, you can build ramps and staircases as well. If you find yourself in a valley and you must reach higher ground quickly, then build a staircase for yourself. Build a ramp to navigate from one tower to another. There are plenty of ways in which the structures you build in this game can save your life in a critical moment. Once the map starts to shrink, it might be a good idea to move inwards and build a sniper nest for yourself.

Tip #2 Landing spot matters

If you jump right into the middle of a vast construction that has plenty of loot, you will get yourself killed quickly. It is foolish to do this because all the other players will do the same. Instead, head for the middle or the far edge of the map in the game.

Tip #3 Loot Lake

In the middle of the map, there is a spot known as Loot Lake, and it is worth the gamble. The lake island has a house that contains two golden chests. The boat on the lake has one golden chest. The tricky bit that you should overcome is the speed. When you wade through water, your speed will reduce to half, and it is in open terrain. If there are a few players on either side, you will put yourself in mortal danger. If any other players drop near the lake, avoid the island at all costs. It is a great spot to get loot, but it is slightly risky.

Tip #4 Anarchy Acres

At the end of the map, near the Storm's edge, there is a spot known Anarchy Acres. You will have to wait longer to jump on the bus if you want to land at this spot. It might be a slight disadvantage if you have to wait for longer than others. However, if everyone drops off the bus before you do, you can quickly secure a couple of good weapons and healing items. These are two great spots to avoid any early campers. You will learn more about proper landing spots in the coming chapters. Regardless of where you land, keep in mind that the map will shrink, and buildings tend to become more dangerous as you progress through the game.

Tip #5 - Learn to stay alive

Your aim in the game shouldn't be just to survive but to win. If you hide correctly and choose your battles carefully, you can quickly make it into the top 20. However, is it really how you want to play the game? It isn't difficult to keep out of sight, but if you don't use it to snipe or scope for better locations, you are just wasting time. You should scout the areas that others scavenge and kill those players who got their hands on a lot of loot. You can build a sniper's nest to get a clear line of sight to any of the players nearby. You can wait near the edge of the safe zone and take all those out while they rush in when the storm advances. You can stay on the edge of the Storm and move only when you have to. When you do this, you reduce the chances of being shot from the back. Regardless of the strategy you use, you have to engage in a firefight, if you want to win.

Tip #6 Sound Cues

You can hear movement when someone sprints, and it's a telltale sign that there is another player in the vicinity. It also warns you when someone else spots you. If you pay attention to the sound cues, you can save yourself. Whenever you fire a weapon or when someone else fires a weapon, you can hear a loud noise. Not just that, even chests have a peculiar sound. Sometimes, you will have to smash up a wall or a floor to find a chest.

Tip #7 Use the Bush

Well, do you know what a Bush disguise is in Fortnite Battle Royale? If you don't, then read on to learn more about this brilliant disguise technique. There is a new Bush consumable in the game, and it does make for hilarious outdoor encounters in Fortnite Battle Royale. It is not just about getting your hands on the Bush in the game; the effectiveness of the consumable depends on how well you can use it.

There are a couple of things that you should keep in mind before you can use this disguise. The Bush is a legendary consumable. So, it means that it is somewhat rare to find and you can use it once. Whenever the Bush takes on any damage, it will disappear quickly. Damage doesn't necessarily have to be from firefights; even any damage from the Storm will destroy the Bush disguise. Once the disguise wears off, it will reveal your character to all the other players around.

You can find the Bush only in chests and supply drops in the Battle Royale game. If you want to obtain a Bush disguise, then stay alert and search in all the locations where chests spawn. Stay alert when you near a chest, in case some other player also has a similar idea. You can even obtain this item from another opponent. When you kill a foe, you can loot the body for any supplies, and if the character happens to have a Bush disguise on him, then it is yours. It can be quite tricky to obtain because once a player gets the Bush disguise, they will use it instead immediately. You cannot carry more than one Bush item in your inventory. So, use this only when you trek in the outdoor areas of the game.

Once you obtain a Bush disguise, you have to try and make the most of it. You can use it only for a limited period, and you also have to use it as soon as you can. Well, here are a couple of tips that you can keep in mind when you use the Bush camouflage.

You should stay outdoors. If you stay indoors, you cannot use the camouflage. It is quite an obvious thing. You cannot don the Bush disguise and wait in a building. Bushes are found outdoors, and the idea is to merge with the outdoors to avoid enemies. If you use the disguise indoors, it will make you an easy target. So, think like a Bush and stay outdoors.

There are different types of bushes in the Fortnite Royale Game. Select the bushes so that your Bush disguise will help you to merge with the background. Make sure that you don't stay out and you blend in with the surroundings. If you don't blend in with the surroundings, it will give your location away.

You should stay still when you don the disguise. Lots of people make this mistake. A bush doesn't move around, does it? Well, neither should you. The more you restrict your movement, the better your chances are to catch your foe off-guard.

You should crouch when you use the Bush. If you stand up, you risk exposing your character to others. It is best to crouch at all times when you use this item.

The Storm can damage your Bush disguise, so you have to avoid the Storm at all costs. Keep an eye on the map to avoid a Storm.

Chapter Four: Strategies

Fortnite Battle Royale and Player Unknown's Battlegrounds are quite similar in the manner that they both vie for world domination. However, there are a lot of differences between these two games. When you start the game, you will have a pickaxe with you, and you can use it to collect the resources you need. You can use the wood, metal and bricks you harvest to build stairs, walls and platforms in the game.

There is one strategy that can help you to come out on top in this game. This strategy is known as the "stairway to heaven." In this strategy, you have to make sure that you land in an area with a lot of trees and other resources that you can mine. Mine as much as you can and grab the weapons and healing resources on your way. You have to move towards the outer edge of the safe zone and start to build. Build the stairway as high as you can, until you are above the rest of the game and no other player can notice you. Once you do this, you can start to build a plank towards the safe zone in the game. In the end, you might notice that there are a handful of players and the height the plank is able to provide you a good vantage point. If you are lucky, you can avoid a lot of firefights. If you can manage to gather all the resources you need quickly, you can start to build immediately. You can use this tactic whenever you want to, either at the beginning of the game or even mid-way through the game. However, this isn't an infallible strategy. Your opponents can shoot you down if they look up, especially if they have rocket launchers. It is likely that you might even run into another player while on the plank. If you aren't careful, you can also plummet to your death or run out of the necessary resources.

The Storm is poisonous, and it hinders your buildings and constructions, but did you know that you could use it to your advantage as well? The Storm does shrink the map, but it gives you sufficient time to get inside the Eye and even if you notice that you are in a danger zone, your health doesn't drain quickly. So, the Storm isn't that lethal in the first couple of rounds. However, in series 4 or 5, the Storm is deadly, and you should carefully monitor your health and don't get trapped in it. When the map shrinks, you will have to move toward the center of the map, and the player count also decreases accordingly. You can reduce the chances of an attack if you make sure that your back is toward the Storm. It is quite unlikely that a player will be present at the edge of the Storm. So, keep an eye on where the Eye of the Storm is present and the time that's left before the Storm starts the Shrinking phase. You can plan your route and make sure that you have all the necessary supplies.

Chapter Five: All about the Weapons

In this section, you will learn all the different weapons available in the game and much more.

Did you know that the weapons available in Fortnite Battle Royale belong to different tiers? If you notice, different arms are of different colors. There are five colors, and these are gray, green, blue, purple and orange. The color grey signifies a common weapon, green represents different weapons, blue means rare weapons, purple stands for epic weapons and orange for legendary weapons.

The scroll wheel feature of this game helps you to manage your inventory in the game. There are five inventory slots and a couple of medical supplies when you begin the game.

The sniper rifles are the best weapons in the game. If you can manage to obtain a legendary sniper, you will have an upper hand over all your enemies in firefights. When you use this weapon, you can knock a player out in one hit, and it is quite helpful. You can't attach any other features to your weapons, so you don't have to worry about any attachments. Your aim should be to collect as many powerful weapons as you can.

There are two types of weapons in Fortnite Battle Royale - hitscan and projectile. These travel differently, and it is thus important for you to know the difference. Hitscan weapons fire instantly and hit the center instantly. On the other hand, projectile weapons take some time to travel across the battlefield. An example of such a weapon is a grenade launcher. In the case of the projectile weapon, therefore, you need to anticipate where your enemy will be moving in a couple of seconds and then fire there. This will help you establish the right kind of connection. Again, this might seem a little obvious – but when you are looking to become an expert in a short period, it is these little things that we tend to forget.

As soon as you get started with the game, among the first things you should attempt to do is securing an assault rifle and a shotgun. You don't want to be caught empty-handed soon after you've started the game, so definitely do not forget to do this. You want the dual advantage of having a good weapon up close as well as for a range. Once you have these, you can start being more selective with your weapon choices. The other weapons will follow after you've eliminated a competitor or through loots, but don't forget to have these.

If you have a moment to do this, what you also want to do is change the order of the guns in your inventory, so this combination of weapons is next to each other. Thus, you will only have to press the button once to switch between them, which will undoubtedly be useful in the case of combat situations. Make sure you are in a safe space before you do this though, you do not want to be ambushed while you were dealing with your inventory.

Also, be ready to switch as soon as you can, depending on the situation you are in. Remember to always switch to a shotgun right before you enter a house, so you can attack in a closed space. Again, right before you leave the house, you can switch back to an assault rifle so you can fire better in the open space.

It's important to remember that DPS (damage per second) is an important consideration to make when you think about switching weapons. Within the same class of weapons, the higher type is better because the increase in rarity increases the level of damage it can cause. However, it is not that simple when you are looking at different gun types. What you then want to look at is how the damage and fire rate combine to create the DPS. While the weapons might not differ on those stats in isolation, they will show you what to prefer when looking at the DPS.

In addition to this, it also depends on how much faith you have in the accuracy of your shot. If you are an accurate shot, you can choose damage because you know you can successfully inflict that without making too many errors. On the other hand, if you are unsure if you will land a hit, choose DPS instead. This will help you hit your opponent enough times for it to count, even if the gaps between getting those hits are longer.

How do you calculate the damage a weapon can inflict? What is this number and why is it important? When you look at a weapon, it has a value affixed to it that helps you to understand its power. Some weapons pack quite a punch but fire slowly. You have to consider the magazine size as well. DPS refers to damage per second, and it can also help you to select a suitable weapon. So, let us take a look at the different weapons available in this game.

All Assault Rifles and their stats

M16

It has a DPS of 176. The damage it inflicts is 32. It falls under the "common" category of weapons and has a magazine size of 30.

M16

It has a DPS of 181. The damage it inflicts is 32. It falls under the "uncommon" category of weapons and has a magazine size of 30.

M16

It has a DPS of 192. The damage it inflicts is 33. It falls under the "rare" category of weapons and has a magazine size of 30.

SCAR

It has a DPS of 203. The damage it inflicts is 37. It falls under the "epic" category of weapons and has a magazine size of 30.

SCAR

It has a DPS of 214. The damage it inflicts is 39. It falls under the "legendary" category of weapons and has a magazine size of 30.

Scoped Rifle

It has a DPS of 80. The damage it inflicts is 23. It falls under the "rare" category of weapons and has a magazine size of 20.

Scoped Rifle

It has a DPS of 84. The damage it inflicts is 23. It falls under the "epic" category of weapons and has a magazine size of 20.

Semi-Auto Rifle

It has a DPS of 118. The damage it inflicts is 29. It falls under the "common" category of weapons and has a magazine size of 30.

Semi-Auto Rifle

It has a DPS of 122. The damage it inflicts is 30. It falls under the "uncommon" category of weapons and has a magazine size of 30.

Semi-Auto Rifle

It has a DPS of 203. The damage it inflicts is 37. It falls under the "rare" category of weapons and has a magazine size of 30.

All Pistols and their stats

Here is a detailed list of all the pistols available in the game along with their DPS, magazine size, and the base damage they inflict.

Revolver

It has a DPS of 48. The damage it inflicts is 54. It falls under the "common" category of weapons and has a magazine size of 6.

Revolver

It has a DPS of 51. The damage it inflicts is 57. It falls under the "uncommon" category of weapons and has a magazine size of 6.

Revolver

It has a DPS of 54. The damage it inflicts is 60. It falls under the "rare" category of weapons and has a magazine size of 6.

Semi-Auto Handgun

It has a DPS of 155. The damage it inflicts is 23. It falls under the "common" category of weapons and has a magazine size of 16.

Semi-Auto Handgun

It has a DPS of 162. The damage it inflicts is 24 points. It falls under the "uncommon" category of weapons and has a magazine size of 16.

Semi-Auto Handgun

It has a DPS of 169. The damage it inflicts is 25 points. It falls under the "rare" category of weapons and has a magazine size of 16.

All Shotguns and their stats

Pump Shotgun

It has a DPS of 63. The damage it inflicts is 90 points. It falls under the "common" category of weapons and has a magazine size of 5.

Pump Shotgun

It has a DPS of 66. The damage it inflicts is 95 points. It falls under the "uncommon" category of weapons and has a magazine size of 5.

Semi-Auto Shotgun

It has a DPS of 100. The damage it inflicts is 67 points. It falls under the "uncommon" category of weapons and has a magazine size of 8.

Semi-Auto Shotgun

It has a DPS of 105. The damage it inflicts is 70 points. It falls under the "rare" category of weapons and has a magazine size of 8.

Semi-Auto Shotgun

It has a DPS of 111. The damage it inflicts is 73 points. It falls under the "epic" category of weapons and has a magazine size of 8.

All Sniper Rifles and Stats

If you want to take out your foes from afar, then you need sniper rifles.

Bolt Action Sniper AWP

It has a DPS of 35. The damage it inflicts is 105 points. It falls under the "rare" category of weapons and has a magazine size of 1.

Bolt Action Sniper AWP

It has a DPS of 37. The damage it inflicts is 110 points. It falls under the "epic" category of weapons and has a magazine size of 1.

Semi-Auto Sniper

It has a DPS of 75. The damage it inflicts is 63 points. It falls under the "epic" category of weapons and has a magazine size of 10.

Semi-Auto Sniper

It has a DPS of 80. The damage it inflicts is 66 points. It falls under the "legendary" category of weapons and has a magazine size of 10.

All SMGs and their stats

Here is a list of all the SMGs that are currently available in the Fortnite Battle Royale game.

Submachine Gun

The DPS it boasts of is 150. The damage it inflicts is 10. It falls under the "common" category of weapons and has a magazine size of 25.

Submachine Gun

The DPS it boasts of is 165. The damage it inflicts is 11. It falls under the "uncommon" category of weapons and has a magazine size of 25.

Tactical SMG

The DPS it boasts of is 140. The damage it inflicts is 14. It falls under the "uncommon" category of weapons and has a magazine size of 30.

Tactical SMG

The DPS it boasts of is 150. The damage it inflicts is 15. It falls under the "rare" category of weapons and has a magazine size of 30.

Tactical SMG

The DPS it boasts of is 160. The damage it inflicts is 16. It falls under the "epic" category of weapons and has a magazine size of 30.

Tactical SMG

The DPS it boasts of is 170. The damage it inflicts is 17. It falls under the "legendary" category of weapons and has a magazine size of 30.

Rocket Launchers and their stats

Here is a list of all the rocket launchers in the game and their stats.

Rocket Launcher

The DPS it boasts of is 82. The damage it inflicts is 110. It falls under the "rare" category of weapons and has a magazine size of 1.

Rocket Launcher

The DPS it boasts of is 87. The damage it inflicts is 116. It falls under the "epic" category of weapons and has a magazine size of 1.

Rocket Launcher

The DPS it boasts of is 91. The damage it inflicts is 121. It falls under the "legendary" category of weapons and has a magazine size of 1.

Grenade launchers and their stats

There are two types of grenade launchers in this game, and the only difference is the damage they inflict.

Grenade Launcher

The DPS it boasts of is 100. The damage it inflicts is 100. It falls under the "rare" category of weapons and has a magazine size of 6.

Grenade Launcher

The DPS it boasts of is 110. The damage it inflicts is 110. It falls under the "legendary" category of weapons and has a magazine size of 6.

Best Weapons

If you want to become an excellent Fortnite Battle Royale player, you should learn to make good use of any weapon you find. However, some weapons are better than the rest. If you are new to this game, then you should know the top 5 weapons in this game. When you analyze the capabilities of a weapon, you should consider the DPS, damage, extent and impact of the weapon. If you have to decide whether a weapon is good or not, consider these numbers. Not just that, pay attention to the rarity of the weapon as well. In this section, you will learn the five best weapons in Fortnite Royale Battle.

Assault Rifle (SAR)

The DPS of this weapon is 122.5, the damage it inflicts is 35 points, the range is 1, and the impact is 28. The assault rifle is one of the most potent weapons in Fortnite. It is a rare weapon and has the most accuracy in this game. It isn't for a close-range shot. Well, it is a sniper and snipers work best from a distance. If you want a clear shot from a distance, then this should be your go-to weapon.

Semi-Automatic Shotgun (SAS)

It boasts of a 122.5 DPS, the damage it inflicts is of 35 points, the range is 1, and the impact is 28. SAS is available in two rarities in the game, and these are unusual and rare categories. There is a pump shotgun in this game, but it serves different purposes. Regardless of the rarity of the SAS, it is a much better weapon than a pump shotgun. The pump shotgun has a DPSS of 63-66.5. If you want to shoot someone at close range, then the pump variant is better. The SAS is more versatile than the pump shotgun.

Sniper Rifle

It has a DPS of 34, 36, and 38. The damage it inflicts is 105, 110, and 116 respectively. The range of all the sniper rifle variants is 1. The impact, however, varies between 360 and 396, and it depends on the rarity of the weapon. It is a powerful and precise sniper rifle. It comes with a bolt-action mechanism that is quite reliable. However, the speed at which it fires is slower than the previous two weapons. In the Battle Royale mode, this weapon causes a lot of damage.

Assault rifle (SCAR)

It has a DPS of 203 and 214. The damage it inflicts is 37 and 39 respectively. The range of all these weapons is 1. According to the rarity of the weapon, the impact ranges between 29 and 31. Assault rifles are quite crucial in any shooting game, and it is the same in Fortnite Battle Royale as well. This weapon should always be there in your arsenal, and it should be in the first slot in your inventory. You can start with a standard variant, and after a while, you will find the SCAR variant of the assault rifle that is legendary. The epic and legendary options of assault rifles cause more damage than the other variants.

Rocket Launcher

The DPS it offers ranges between 82 and 90. According to the level of rarity, the damage it can inflict varies from 110 to 121 points. There is a lot of debate about the power of a rocket launcher and a grenade launcher. However, it all boils down to the damage stats, and a rocket launcher has better stats. A rocket launcher only has one round, whereas a grenade launcher has six rounds. If you have to blast your foe's buildings to bits and want to do so quickly, then the rocket launcher is the best option.

Chapter Six: Best Places to Loot

If you want to gather as many supplies as possible, then you should know the best places to loot. However, how do you know where these locations are? The best loot usually spawns at the regular locations, and these locations don't change. Most of these locations are present towards the upper part of the island on the map. So, if you can manage to jump off in one of the northern spots, then you can find a decent number of chests to plunder. In this section, you will learn the best places to loot in Fortnite: Battle Royale game.

Waling Wood #1

The first spot that you should explore is the spot right above the Wailing Wood in the G2 block of the game map. You will notice a tall wooden tower with multiple floors. You can find some of the best loot in the chests present here. The first chest you will come across is stowed away behind the wall on the second floor of the tower. You can see the chest emanate a pale golden glow through the planks of the wall. Another chest is present on the top of the tower. Apart from this, you will also come across a lot of random loot strewn across the tower. If you want to pillage the area, you need a set of stairs to get there. So, make sure that your inventory has sufficient wood before you can loot the tower.

Wailing Wood #2

The next location you should check for loot is the ice-cream truck that appears above the wooden tower in the previous area. It spawns in the upper segment of the F2 block on the game map. You will find a chest near the truck. However, at times another chest can also appear on the top of the truck. So, don't forget to check the top of the truck as well. Once you do this, head down the hill and plunder the two houses for more ammo and supplies.

Anarchy Acres

When you move towards the central part of the map from the previous location, you will come across a river and a bridge that connects it to a farming area and eventually the Anarchy Acres. It is a brilliant place to look for chests as well as boxes of ammo that are usually hidden in the basement or somewhere near the bridge. Check all the trucks that spawn in this area. The Anarchy Acres is one of the best spots to loot, while you do this, make sure that you take a couple of shield potions, and it will make you ready to face any other players in battle.

Pleasant Park

In the northern part of the Fortnite Battle Royale, the best spot to plunder is Pleasant Park. This spot has plenty of houses, but there is one building that deserves a special mention. You will come across a modern three-story building towards the southeastern part of Pleasant Park. In this building, you will find a chest inside the garage. Once you see the chest, use your pickaxe to plunder it. However, don't leave after you loot the chest. Look around the house, check the upper floors, and you will undoubtedly find a couple of supplies and weapons that you should pick up.

Flush Factory

The Flush Factory is present at the bottom of the map, and it boasts of good loot as well. You should concentrate on the southern part of the building, and you will find a large platform. A chest always spawns in this location. However, it doesn't mean that you ignore the factory. Go and check the inside and outside areas of the factory carefully. You will undoubtedly find something that you can use.

Well, these are all the best spots that you will find excellent loot at. Make sure that you memorize these locations. It is easier to gather supplies when you don't have to look at the map consistently, and you can get there faster.

Chapter Seven: Best Landing Spots

Your success rate in the Battle Royale mode depends a lot on the way you start the game. If you land in an area with nothing other than a pistol in your arsenal, you are in for a lot of trouble. The game is fast-paced, so you should make sure that you land in a right spot to collect as many weapons and supplies as you possibly can. A good landing spot will help you gather the necessary supplies. You need to understand that all the landing spots aren't equal regarding the loot they offer. There are a couple of landing spots that are quite favorable and the others not so much. Regardless of where you land, make sure that there is something worthwhile near you. If you are a beginner, then don't let the different names scare you. Here is a list of all the best landing spots in this game.

Monstrous Motel

The Monstrous Motel is quite low-key when you compare it to Anarchy Acres that is present right next to it. It is present in the D2 quadrant on the map. Other than the signboard with its name, this structure is preferably bland to look at. However, it does have the decent loot to offer in the two houses next to it and the truck that's present near the pool. Don't forget to look in the rooms. The design makes it tricky to predict any enemy movements nearby precisely.

Anarchy Acres

The Anarchy Acres are present in the F2 quadrant on the map. It is amongst the best places to loot in the game and is, therefore, an excellent spot to land. The farmhouse on Anarchy Acres offers at least two chests with lots of proper supplies. You should land above the bathroom in the farmhouse and break into the building from there, or you can even go into the attic. You can choose either of these routes but listen carefully for the hum that chests make. Once you loot the house, you can climb on the roof and assess the area around the house. Make sure that you check the small ridge at the back of the house. If you are lucky, you can find a chest that is hidden behind the wooden paneling.

Tilted Towers

The Titled Towers are present in the D6 quadrant in the game. This location offers prime loot, and it, therefore, attracts a lot of players. If you want to land in this location, then you should land in the low house near the towers. This spot isn't used frequently and is amongst the safer options available. You can find a couple of chests on different floors, and you should go to the underground garage to hunt for more loot. You can see the garage from one of the rear windows in the house. You can find a hidden chest or two with a little bit of digging. Once you gather all the loot, just get out of Tilted Towers as soon as you can.

Hell Hill

The Hell Hill is the unofficial name for the hill that overlooks Fatal Fields. If you land here, you should prepare yourself for a firefight or two. It is a high vantage point, and therefore you shouldn't overlook it. If you want to look for chests, then check the basketball course, the house, and the bridge to nowhere. You can even harvest plenty of materials from the cars nearby and then move on to the next location.

Car Crevice

It is slightly tricky to land at this spot because of all the hills around it. If you want a low-activity place with a chance to loot a couple of chests nearby, then this is an ideal spot. There is chest within the house that has a car on its roof and also on the hangman's galley. From there, you can quickly head towards either Shifty Shafts or Greasy Groove.

Fancy Factories

It is present in G6 quadrant on the map and is a great spot to land. It is near Dusty and Retail. When you decide to land here, make sure that you land on the highest factory because it offers the best loot on its roof. You can then make your way down the factory and find some loot in the buildings nearby. If you want to land here, you should expect a little combat. It is an excellent spot to try some traps as well. However, be mindful of Retail Row, which is next door.

Retail Row

It is present in the H6 quadrant in the map, and you can practice your craft without getting overwhelmed. The Retail Row is a very busy aware, so be quite alert while you are in this location. Most of the players tend to head for the houses. You can instead head towards the shops and check for loot. There are plenty of spots here where you can come across a chest or two. Once you have plenty of supplies, you can head towards the houses and kill any other players who come along your way. If you aren't feeling too brave and want to avoid a fight, then you can head towards Fancy Factories.

Tomato Town- Bridge

It is present in the H4 quadrant in the game. This spot was initially overlooked but is slowly gaining popularity. However, it isn't a surprise given all the possibilities it has to offer. The two places that most of the player's head for are the house or the tunnel. You should instead land on the bridge. You can find a couple of good weapons near the bridge. Make sure that you check the underneath of the chest for a hidden chest. It is also a great spot to harvest some bricks and stone. Once you have sufficient stock, you can head towards the gunfire, if you want to.

Snobby Shores

It is present in the A5 quadrant on the map in Fortnite Battle Royale. Not a lot of people seem too keen to land on the spot near the coastline. However, you shouldn't overlook it because it offers a lot of loot. You will find a chest or two in almost all the houses. You should check the underground bunkers to see some interesting loot. It is a little far away from the circle, but the loot it offers might be worth taking.

Chapter Eight: Leveling Tips

There are different aspects of the leveling system in Fortnite Battle Royale. For starters, when you earn experience points your season level progresses. When your season level increases, you gain Battle Stars. These Battle Stars help you to advance your Battle Pass, and it helps you to unlock different goodies that help you to advance through ranks and come to new tiers. All this might confuse a new player, and therefore, you will find all the information you need about the leveling system in this section. The first aspect that you need to learn is to gain experience points through regular play in the game. Then you will learn Battle Stars and the Pass.

There are different ways in which you can gain experience points or XP. You can earn these points whenever you play the game. There are a couple of factors that determine the XP you gain. The longer you stay in the game, the more XP you will receive at the end of the match. The higher is your position in the game, the higher XP you will win. Even the number of kills you manage will increase your XP. Also, when you reach a specific milestone on the Battle Pass, you will receive bonus XP. Not just that, you will even receive an XP modifier that helps you to double your gains.

If you complete any of the regular challenges, you can earn XP. All these points will accumulate over time, and it will lead to an increase in your rank. Daily challenges are rotating tasks, and the primary objective is to make a kill with a specific weapon.

Battle Stars are the unit of progress that helps you to move through different tiers in the game. The number of Battle Stars you earn will be present in the Battle Pass. Before the start of a season, every player gets a Battle Pass. It might seem a little tricky to process all this. However, it is quite simple, and it isn't complicated at all. When your season level increases you gain a Battle Star. When you reach the five-level milestone, like Level 5, Level 15 and Level 25 and so on, you will receive five bonus Battle Stars. However, keep in mind that there are two types of Battle Pass and these are the free and the premium ones.

The free version only offers a set number of cosmetic items that you can unlock during the season. Whereas the premium one is a paid for a pass and it contains way more items than the free pass. The good news is that you don't have to buy a premium pass immediately. You can check your progress through the game and buy a premium pass later on in the season. When you buy a premium pass, you are entitled to additional rewards. At a specific tier in the Battle Pass you will even unlock an XP boost that helps you to rise through the ranks and in turn, increases the Battle Stars you earn. You can also use V-bucks to skip through a tier if you want. It costs about 150 V-bucks to skip through a tier at any time. It is a good purchase, especially if you want a head start in the game.

You must complete the challenges that are available. To check the challenges merely click on the Inspect Challenges button. When you want to loot a chest, you will crack it open. It is an essential part of the game, and you will do this all through the game. Well, the good news is that when you open chests and crates of ammo, it helps to level up. Try to stay in the game for as long as you possibly can to increase your XP. You can stay for long in the game, if you choose your battles wisely, dodge fights, and stay away from areas with high activity. Even when you kill your foes, your XP will increase.

Chapter Nine: Building Tips

In this section, you will learn different building tips that will help you along your way in the game.

Break things down

The first thing that you should do in Fortnite Battle Royale, apart from making sure that no one kills you is to build up your stockpile of different materials. The various elements available are wood, bricks and metal. You should have sufficient supplies of each of these materials at all times. Wood is the weakest material and metal is the strongest of the lot. You will find a lot of metal from the cars in Flush Factory. As you start to progress through the game, having sufficient supplies can decide your fate in the game. Especially when you are stuck in a fight, your ability to build a wall immediately can save you at the right time. There are plenty of things that you can break down to harvest building supplies. Well, there is one thing that you shouldn't waste your effort on, and that's shipping containers. It isn't worth it to break large shipping containers like the ones you find in Dusty Depot. They take a long time to break down, and the reward you receive isn't worth the effort you put into the process.

Take high ground

It is a good idea to run for high ground whenever you can. It is a useful strategy because it provides you a good vantage point for all the other players in the game. If you have to fight someone, would you rather be at the top of a hill or the bottom of it? If you take the high ground, it will allow you to peak into the enemy bases, and you can get a jump on them quickly. If luck favors you, you can even get a rough idea of where the map shrinks, and it will give you a chance to construct a base before anyone else gets there. You will be in for a nasty surprise if you see a giant tower just waiting for you, especially after you complete a firefight or when you escape the storm by the skin of your teeth. If you build steps to your opponent's base, you have the element of surprise in your favor. It is a good strategy if you play in a team. Your team members can distract the enemy, and you can kill the enemy in the meanwhile.

Build stairs

Stairs are an essential part of the gameplay in Fortnite Battle Royale. They will help you reach specific points that would have otherwise been inaccessible. How on Earth can you reach the top of an enemy tower or base, without stairs to get you there? Stairs not only provide access, but they are an excellent place to hide, and they provide cover a well. The most straightforward option is to build steps with wood, but then these steps are quite weak as well. Structures cannot float in this game, so if you don't have a base, you lose the structure you build as well. Remember that it is hard to defend yourself form a stair attack. Structures are at their most vulnerable within a couple of moments of their construction. If your enemy gets a hint of what you are up to, it might spell trouble for you.

Fortify the base

You might be pretty excited to start building right away. However, you have to make sure that the foundation you build is strong enough to sustain any damage in a fight. If your base isn't strong enough, then none of the other constructions will survive. So, before you build, make sure that the foundation is quite sturdy. As mentioned in the previous point, if someone takes out your base, your entire construction will come tumbling down. The best material to build the base structure is metal. You can use wood for the foundation, but it is quite easy to destroy anything made out of wood. You should fortify the base and do this, build a couple of walls around the ground floor of your structure.

Use materials wisely

The map in the game shrinks continuously. You have to be careful of the manner in which you use the resources you gather. It is essential that you invest in resources, but don't use all your resources at once. It might seem entirely exciting to start building a base as soon as you begin to play the game. However, remember that the map shrinks and when it does, you have to move ahead and leave your base behind. If you use all your resources just to build one map, you won't have anything left to construct with as you progress in the game. Instead, try to gather as many resources as you possibly can until the circle gets small enough so that you can build your base. You don't have to create a sprawling base, but you should have the necessary supplies to at least build a decent one when the time comes. If you are lucky enough, then you can quickly identify the spot wherein the map will shrink.

Types of builds in Fortnite Battle Royale

There are different types of structures that you can build in the Battle Royale game. For instance, you can construct stairs that will help you access hills or higher ground. They also give you a good vantage point over those players who are on the ground. You can build a bridge to move from one building to another. However, a bridge will leave you vulnerable when you cross from one structure to another. You can build walls around your character for some fortification. When you build walls to surround yourself, make sure that you include a staircase within. It might take a while to do this, but it does give you a high vantage point to take out your foes. You should probably construct a roof if you want to protect yourself from grenades.

Build for movement

A building not only provides you a secure base, but it also gives you different options for movement. You can build platforms and ramps to navigate across cliffs and hills. These structures will also help to break your fall when you move along high structures. Well, if you want a vantage point and there isn't one that's readily available, you can build one for yourself.

<u>Build bases to heal and collect</u>

If you want to gather material or you want a spot to recover, without the fear of being under attack, then build a base to help facilitate this process. It will help to keep the enemies away, at least for a little while, as you go on with the game. When you take some time to heal, make sure that you build a structure with three walls and a ramp. It might give the impression that it is a structure build during battle and they might leave you and your "abandoned" structure alone.

Build wider

It might take a while before you get used to this technique. But you might want to consider building wider structures instead of narrow ones. It will lend some stability to different structures like ramps and platforms. You will notice that enemies cannot bring down the entire structure by merely destroying one base. Additionally, it will also offer you some room that you will need to maneuver around your platforms as you please. It also works as a great escape and defense route. At the same time, don't be afraid to abandon your structure, if it's the best option available. You aim to stay alive for as long as you can. You might not be able to fulfill that aim of yours if you aren't ready to give up on a structure every once in a while.

Editing walls help with vision

Well, this tactic might not help you in every situation, but it's still a useful tip that you need to know. When you go into the Edit mode and change the settings of the game, it allows the walls to become transparent from your end. It means that you can know what's going on around you, without exposing yourself. This option comes in handy when you build a metal wall. You can easily avoid being shot by a sniper and can instead take a shot at your foe. Your enemy cannot spot you, but you can observe them and hit them at the right moment.

Chapter Ten: Team Play Tips

There is a duos mode in Fortnite Battle Royale, and it helps to do some diversity to the game and makes it quite enjoyable. A solo play is good too, however, having a partner will be a fantastic change in the game. Not just the duo mode, you can even play as a team in Fortnite Battle Royale. In this section, you will learn specific tips that will help you to make the most of team play.

It is essential to communicate. If you don't talk, you cannot play as a team. Whenever you spot an enemy, relay the same to your teammates through the compass, and it helps to reduce any distractions. If there is any spot that interests you in the vicinity, relay the same to others. Communicate, communicate, and communicate.

Make the most of the time you have in the pre-game lobby to discuss the game plan. Discuss things like where to land, the strategy you will use in the game, and so on. Make a plan of action and follow it once you start the game. You can decide whether you want to play aggressively or passively.

Harvest as much material as you can along the way. You can harvest trees, cars, boulders, pallets, and just about anything for supplies. It is not you, but everyone on your team should do the same.

When you do loot, intimate your teammates about the items you pick or the ones you leave behind.

Maintain a little distance between you and the other members of the team. If you do get killed, the others can continue the game. Help each other in the game, especially with supplies.

Make use of these tips when you play the game to increase your chances of winning. It is a beautiful idea to play as a team. It will help you to increase your chances of winning.

<u>Conclusion</u>

Thank you once again for choosing this book. I hope it proved to be an informative read.

All the information that you will need about Fortnite Battle Royale is provided in this book. The tips are quite simple and will help you to avoid any beginner mistakes. Not just that, it will enable you to play like a pro within no time. Once you grab a copy of this guide, you can easily dominate the game in no time at all! Make use of the information this book provides to improve your chances of winning! Well, the best way to learn is to practice - so, all that you need to do is to download the game and get started!

...and P.S. – if you found this book helpful, please feel free to leave a review at the Product Detail page, or on your Order page. Thank you and all the best!

Sources

https://www.metabomb.net/fortnite-battle-royale/gameplay-guides/fortnite-battle-royale-base-building-design-tips-and-ideas-4

http://in.ign.com/fortnite/116123/news/8-fortnite-battle-royale-tips-from-pro-streamer-gernaderjake

https://www.fortnitetips.com/2018/01/26/guide-harmonious-co-op-play-strangers-fortnite-save-world/

Printed in Great Britain
by Amazon